This book belongs to :

WHAT THIS BOOK DOES:

Provides a boost in self-esteem while helping your child develop a growth mindset.

Enhances your childs ability to cope with intrusive negative thoughts which can cause anxiety and fear.

Helps children build the confidence and resilience they need for day-to-day living.

Strengthens kids' ability to write complete sentences including capitalization and punctuation.

HOW TO USE THIS BOOK:

SECTION ONE: The first 6 pages are for practicing letter writing with guided directionals and letter tracing.

SECTION TWO: 75 pages of affirmations to practice writing. One on each page followed by plenty of lines to practice writing it several times.

SECTION THREE: Blank pages are for practicing writing favorite affirmations from the book or your child can write their own.

HAVE FUN WITH THIS BOOK AND DON'T FORGET, YOU ARE AWESOME!!

A A A A

B B B B

C C C C

D D D D

E E E E

F F F F

G G G G

H H H H

I I I I

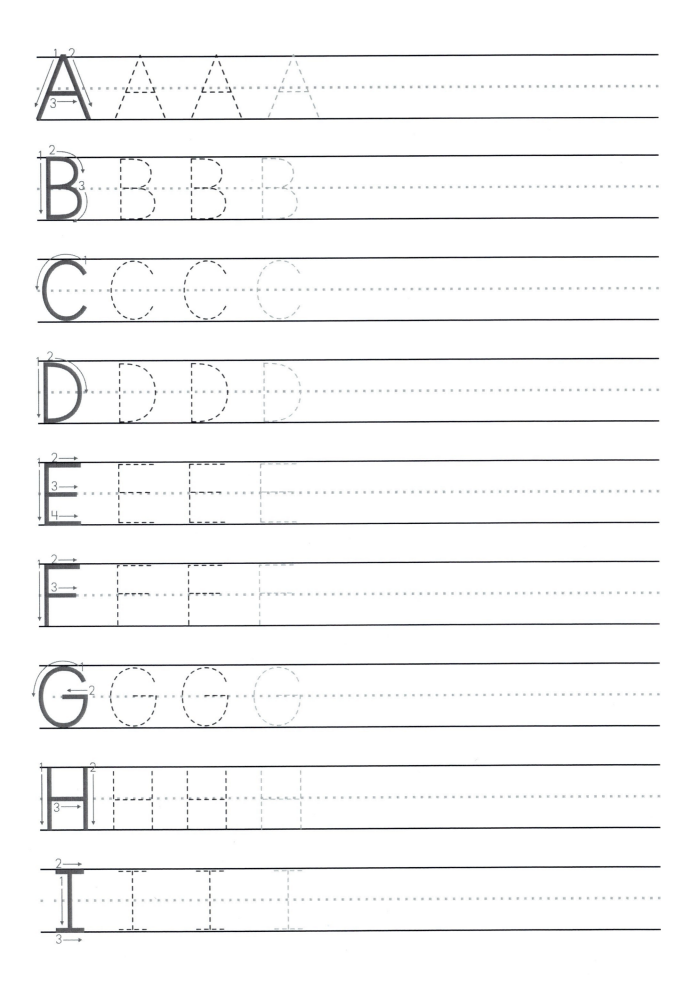

J J J J

K K K K

L L L L

M M M M

N N N N

O O O O

P P P P

Q Q Q Q

R R R R

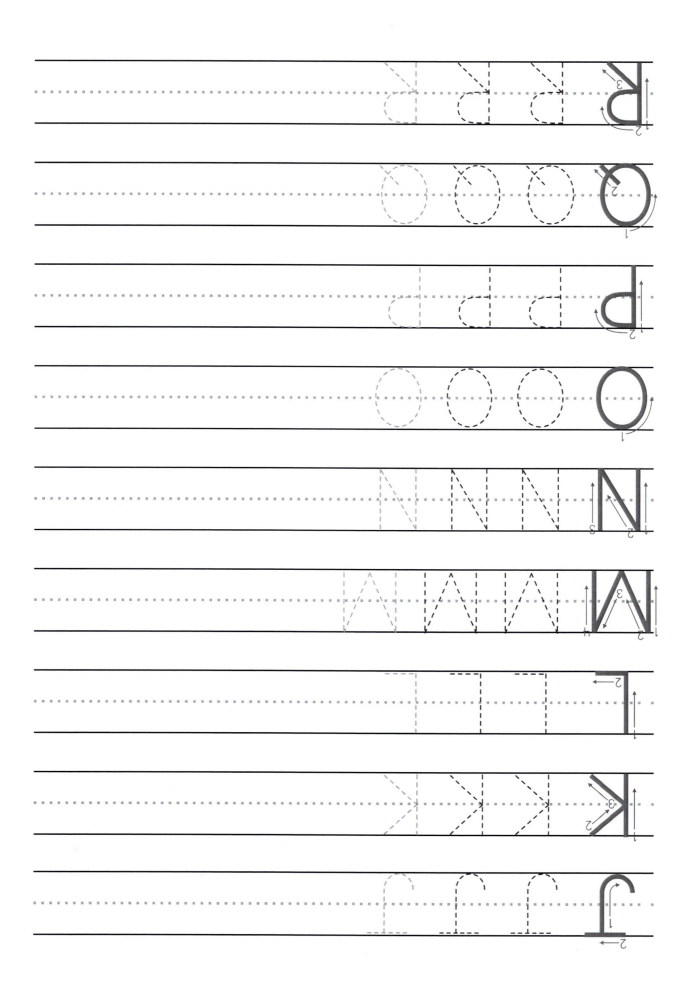

S S S S

T T T T

U U U U

V V V V

W W W W

X X X X

Y Y Y Y

Z Z Z Z

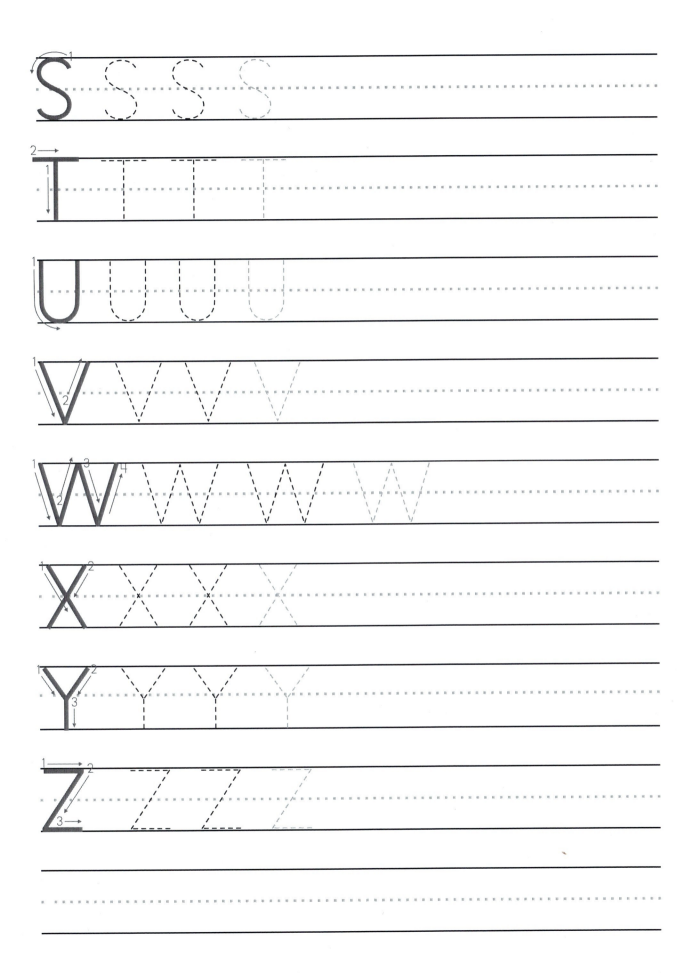

a a a a

b b b b

c c c c

d d d d

e e e e

f f f f

g g g g

h h h h

i i i i

j j j j

k k k k

l l l l

m m m m

n n n n

o o o o

p p p p

q q q q

r r r r

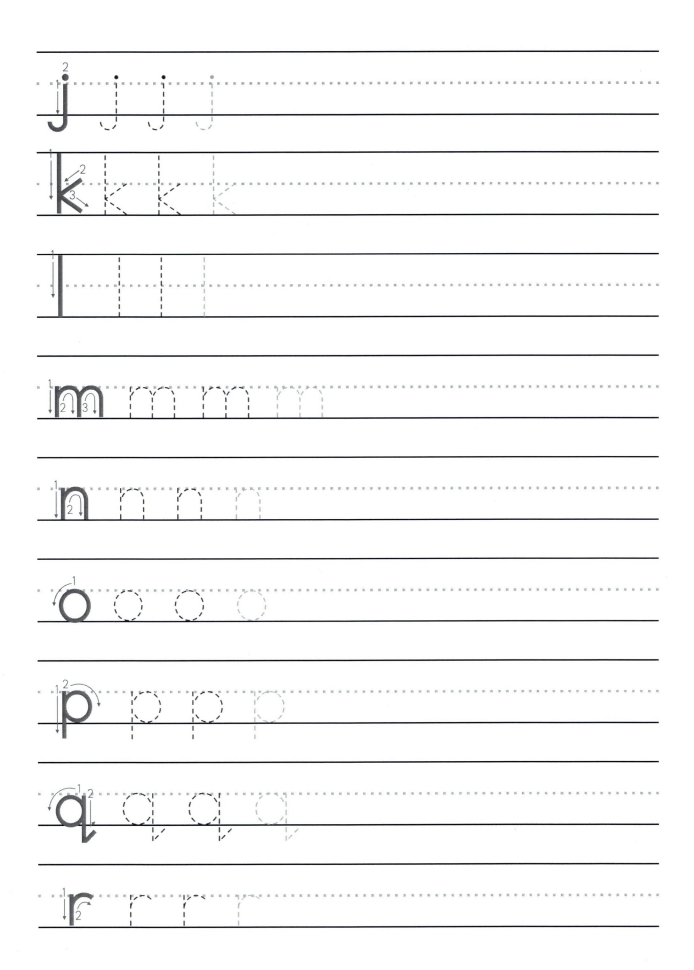

s s s s

t t t t

u u u u

v v v v

w w w w

x x x x

y y y y

z z z z

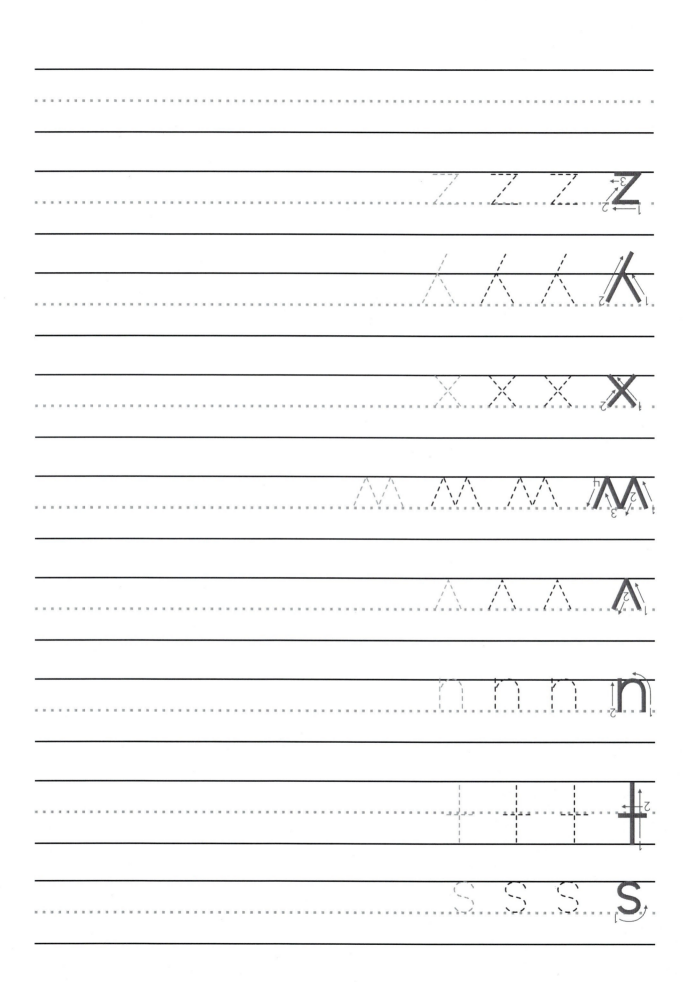

My voice matters.

My voice matters.

I am enough.

I am enough.

I believe in myself.

I believe in myself.

I am brave.

I am brave.

Do you remember a time that you felt brave?
Draw a picture of that time below.

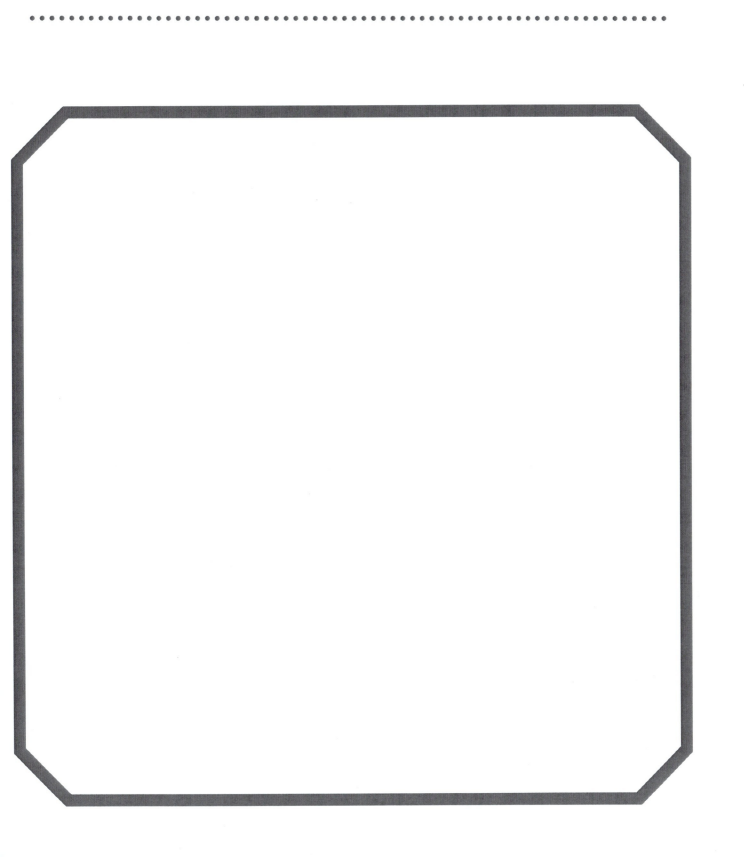

Today I am a
leader.

Today I am a
leader.

I have a big heart.

I have a big heart.

I can do anything.

I can do anything.

I CAN DO
ANYTHING!

I accept who I am.

I accept who I am.

I am important.

I am important.

I am proud of
myself.

I am proud of
myself.

Can you remember a specific time that you were proud of yourself?
Draw a picture of that time in the box below.

I deserve to be
loved.

I deserve to be
loved.

I am a good friend.

I am a good friend.

Differences make

us special.

Differences make

us special.

We’re all different!

I can make a
difference.

I can make a
difference.

I am unique and special.

I am unique and special.

I have many
talents.

I have many
talents.

Which one of your talents is your favorite?
Draw a picture of your awesome talent in the box below.

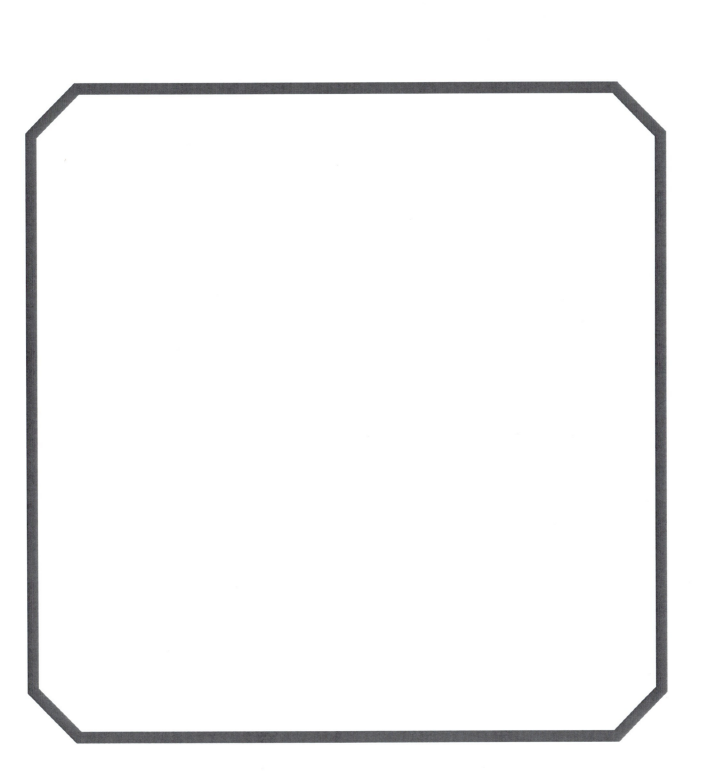

I am loved for
who I am.

I am loved for
who I am.

My ideas are valued.

My ideas are valued.

I am capable.

I am capable.

Today, I will shine.

Today, I will shine.

I LOVE TO LEARN NEW THINGS!

I love to learn
new things.

I love to learn
new things.

I am worthy.

I am worthy.

I have a great personality.

I have a great personality.

My feelings matter.

My feelings matter.

I am a good
listener.

I am a good
listener.

I am wonderful
just as I am.

I am wonderful
just as I am.

My life is beautiful.

My life is beautiful.

I LOVE MAKING NEW FRIENDS!

I love making new friends.

I love making new friends.

I have amazing abilities.

I have amazing abilities.

I can ask for support.

I can ask for support.

I know right from
wrong.

I know right from
wrong.

My future is bright.

My future is bright.

Draw a picture of YOU and your BEST FRIEND in the box below.

I would want to
be my friend.

I would want to
be my friend.

I am a fast
learner.

I am a fast
learner.

My feelings are important.

My feelings are important.

I don't have to
follow the crowd.

I don't have to
follow the crowd.

I choose to think positively.

I choose to think positively.

My happiness is up
to me.

My happiness is up
to me.

I deserve to be happy.

I deserve to be happy.

It is enough to do
my best.

It is enough to do
my best.

I am safe and
cared for.

I am safe and
cared for.

I only compare
myself to myself.

I only compare
myself to myself.

I am an amazing person.

I am an amazing person.

I have a lot to
offer.

I have a lot to
offer.

Hello!

I engage in acts
of kindness.

I engage in acts
of kindness.

My brain is powerful.

My brain is powerful.

I have the words
I need.

I have the words
I need.

I care about
others.

I care about
others.

I am my own
person.

I am my own
person.

My opinion matters.

My opinion matters.

I am smart.

I am smart.

Anything is possible.

Anything is possible.

It's OK to be
different.

It's OK to be
different.

My life is filled
with joy.

My life is filled
with joy.

I am loved.

I am loved.

I love being me.

I love being me.

It's OK to feel all
of my feelings.

It's OK to feel all
of my feelings.

I have unlimited potential.

I have unlimited potential.

I start with a
positive mindset.

I start with a
positive mindset.

Today will be **GREAT!**

I accept myself
for who I am.

I accept myself
for who I am.

My challenges
help me grow.

My challenges
help me grow.

I am confident in
my abilities.

I am confident in
my abilities.

I am a caring person.

I am a caring person.

I forgive myself
for making mistakes.

I forgive myself
for making mistakes.

I am building my future.

I am building my future.

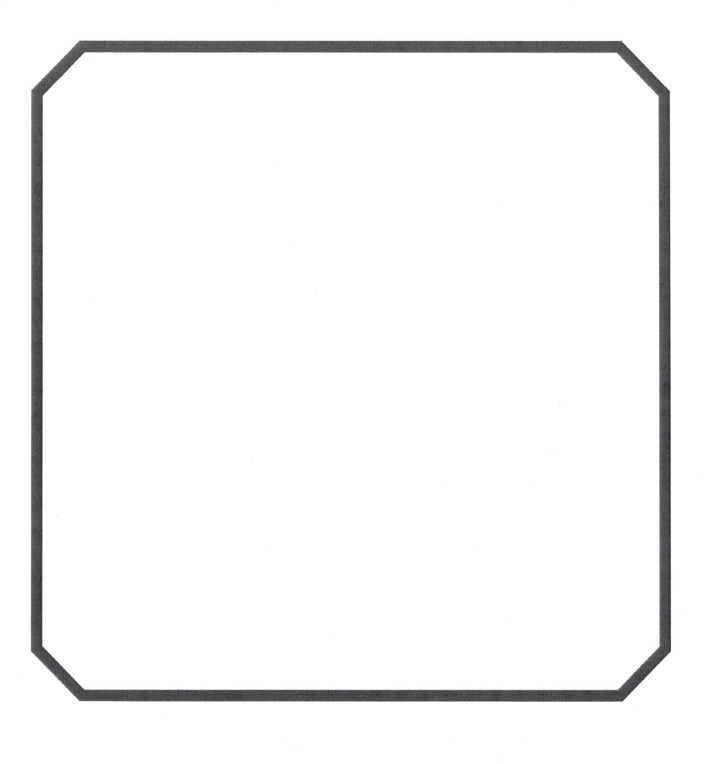

What do you want to be when you are grown up?
A fireman? A scientist? A ballerina?
Draw a picture of it in the box below.

I can be anything
I want to be.

I can be anything
I want to be.

I am full of great
ideas.

I am full of great
ideas.

I have a sharp memory.

I have a sharp memory.

Life is a beautiful
gift.

Life is a beautiful
gift.

Everyday is BEAUTIFUL!

I will make the
most of this day.

I will make the
most of this day.

I am happy and
healthy.

I am happy and
healthy.

I am grateful for
my family.

I am grateful for
my family.

Mistakes help me
to learn and grow.

Mistakes help me
to learn and grow.

I am not afraid of
a challenge.

I am not afraid of
a challenge.

I am so happy to

be alive.

I am so happy to

be alive.

CONGRATULATIONS!

You just wrote some really great words.
Are you feeling terrific?
I hope so because I think you are

TERRIFIC!

For the next section, use the blank lines to re-write your favorite affirmation phrases or write your own.

Be sure to smile while you write.
IT WILL MAKE YOU FEEL HAPPY.
Did you know that even when you feel sad, you can force a smile and it actually makes you feel better?

ISN'T THAT COOL !?!

Made in United States
North Haven, CT
07 December 2024

61898033R00061